Nestlé SMARTIES
Dinosaur Jokes

Smarties titles available

Smarties Beautiful Beasties
Smarties Book of Wizardry
Smarties Chuckle Factory
Smarties Deadly Dinosaurs
Smarties Dinosaurs Jokes
Smarties Guide to the Galaxy
Smarties Hairy Humans
Smarties Hilariously Funny Verse
Smarties How to Draw Cartoons
Smarties How To Make 'Em Laugh Joke Book
Smarties Joke Book
Smarties Knock Knock Jokes
Smarties Practical Jokes
Smarties Puzzle Busters
Smarties Smart Art
Smarties Smart Science
Smarties Travel Teasers
Smarties Wacky World
Smarties Wizard Jokes

Nestlé Smarties Dinosaur Jokes

Illustrations by
DAVID MOSTYN

Compiled by
PETER ELDIN

Robinson Children's Books

Constable & Robinson Ltd
3 The Lanchesters
162 Fulham Palace Road
London W6 9ER
www.constablerobinson.com

First published in the UK by Robinson Children's Books,
an imprint of Constable & Robinson Ltd, 2001

A copy of the British Library Cataloguing in Publication Data
for this title is available from the British Library

ISBN 1-84119-338-0

Printed and bound in the EC

10 9 8 7 6 5 4

Dinosaur Dictionary

This may be a joke book but all the dinosaur names used are those of real creatures that lived many millions of years ago.

So, before we get to the jokes, here is a quick rundown of the dinosaurs that have chosen to appear in this book:

Stegosaurus (steg-o-saw-rus) The largest plated dinosaur. It had two rows of bony (no, not china) plates on its back. Its name means "roof lizard" but you certainly wouldn't want one on your roof.

Iguanodon (ig-wah-no-don) In spite of its size (it was 10 metres long) the Iguanodon was a plant eater. It had an unusual spiked "thumb" – great for hitch hiking!

Triceratops (tri-serra-tops) It had three horns (its name means "three-horned face") and a frill at the back of its head (how frilling!).

Brachiosaurus (brak-ee-o-saw-rus) One of the largest, heaviest and tallest dinosaurs. Its name means "arm lizard" but I bet it wasn't 'armless!

Ichthyosaurus (ik-thee-o-saw-rus) Although reptiles, these sea creatures were very fish-like with fins and a fishy tail.

Mammoth (mam-moth) Ancestor of the elephant and about the same size.

Tyrannosaurus (tie-ran-o-saw-rus) This guy was big! Tyrannosaurus rex was about 14 metres long, its head alone was over a metre in length and it had dagger-like teeth.

Allosaurus (al-o-saw-rus) Had enormous jaws with long teeth – quite a challenge for its dentist.

Archaeopteryx (ark-e-op-ter-iks) With a wing span of 60 cm this feathered dinosaur is regarded as the first bird. Why couldn't the scientists call it "first bird" instead of giving it such a long name?

Brontosaurus (bron-toe-saw-rus) With its eyes and nostrils situated on the top of its small head Brontosaurus could remain almost completely immersed in water – bet that made its skin wrinkle!

Diplodocus (dip-lod-oh-kus) The longest land animal that ever lived. It had a very long neck and tail and lived in swamps.

But that's enough of boring old facts. Let's get on with the jokes . . .

What time is it when you see a dinosaur?
Time to run.

What dinosaur gives you a cheery greeting?
The 'Allo-saurus.

Where would you buy a prehistoric creature?
At a dino-store.

Why don't you see dinosaurs in the zoo?
Because they can't afford the admission.

Why was the Brontosaurus wrinkled?
Did you ever try ironing one?

What do you get if you cross a dinosaur with a
Boy Scout?
A creature that scares old ladies across
the road.

What is pronounced like one letter,
written with three letters, and belongs
to all dinosaurs?
An eye.

What's the difference between a man and
running dinosaur?
One wears trousers, the other pants.

What do you get if you cross a Triceratops
with an owl?
A creature that's ugly but doesn't give a hoot.

What do you get if you cross a Brontosaurus
with fireworks?
Dino-mite.

How did young Archaeopteryx dance?
Chick to chick.

Mr Allosaurus: Gosh! What terrible weather
during the night – thunder, lightning, rain,
the lot!
Mrs Allosaurus: Why didn't you wake me up?
You know I can't sleep during a storm!

What's the time when a dinosaur gets into your bed?
Time to get a new bed.

Where do you find the most Ichthyosaurus?
Between the head and the tail.

What do you call a fish-like reptile that's always scratching?
An itchy-old-sore-us.

The young cavegirl was crying her eyes out.
"What's the matter?" asked her mother.
"My boyfriend and I have just split up," sobbed the girl.
"Never mind," said the mother. "There's plenty more Ichthyosauruses in the sea."

Why did the crossword compiler say "Road in US" when he saw a prehistoric creature on an American road?
Because "Road in US" is an anagram of "dinosaur".

If a dinosaur loses his tail where does he get another one?
At the retail store.

What kind of a bath without water can a
dinosaur take?
A sunbath.

What is the biggest moth in the world?
A Mam-moth.

First Caveman: I was just bitten by a dinosaur.
Second Caveman: Did you put anything on it?
First Caveman: No, he liked it just the way
it was.

What do you call a one-eyed dinosaur?
A D'youthinkesaurus.

Why do Mammoths drink a lot of water?
They are never offered anything else.

If a dinosaur crosses a stream, rolls in the
mud, then crosses back again, what is it?
A dirty double-crosser.

How can you tell a dinosaur from a banana?
Try lifting it. If you can't lift it off the floor
then it's probably a dinosaur.

What do you do when you see a big, fierce
Tyrannosaurus?
Hope he doesn't see you!

What do you call a dinosaur with no legs?
Anything you like, it can't chase you.

Why was the Brontosaurus wrinkled?
It worried a lot.

If a dinosaur was tied to a 20-metre length of
rope how far could it stray?
As far as it likes if the other end of the rope
is not attached to anything.

What's the difference between a hungry
dinosaur and a greedy dinosaur?
One longs to eat, the other eats too long.

What do you call a sweet, charming, good-
natured Tyrannosaurus?
A failure.

What do you call a dinosaur with gravy, potatoes and carrots?
Stew.

What do you call a Stegosaurus with cotton wool in his ears?
Anything you like. He can't hear you.

Why was the Diplodocus a very aristocratic animal?
Because it was a member of "high" society.

Girl on phone: I want to place and advertisement in your newspaper.
Newspaper telephonist: In the Small Ads, Miss?
Girl: Good Heavens, no. I want to sell my pet dinosaur.

Part of the jungle is just two kilometres across. How far can a caveman walk into it? One kilometre. After that he's walking out.

What do you call a dinosaur that's eaten
a dictionary?
A dino-thesaurus.

When the Allosaurus fell in some water, what's
the first thing he did?
Get wet.

What do you get if you cross a Mammoth with a snowman?
A jumbo yeti.

Why did the Tyrannosaurus stand on his head?
He wanted to turn things over in his mind.

What do you get if you cross a dinosaur with a duckling?
A Diplo-duck-us.

What did the Archaeopteryx say when she laid a square egg?
"Ouch!"

What do you get if you cross a parrot with
a dinosaur?
I don't know – but if it talks, you'd better
listen!

Caveman: Can a man be in love with a
Mammoth?
Cavewoman: Of course not!
Caveman: Do you know anyone who wants to buy
a large engagement ring?

What do all dinosaurs and all dinosaur hunters
do at the same time?
They all grow older.

What's the difference between a sabre-toothed tiger and a comma?
The sabre-toothed tiger has claws at the end of its paws and a comma is a pause at the end of a clause.

What do you get if you cross a Mammoth with a skunk?
I don't know, but it wouldn't have any trouble getting a seat on the bus.

Cavewoman: What's the best way to catch an Ichthyosaurus?
Caveman: Get someone to throw one to you.

"Can I help you?" asked the tailor when the Iguanodon walked into his shop.
"Yes, I'd like to see a suit that will fit me," said the Iguanodon.
"So would I," wailed the tailor.

Why did the sabre-toothed tiger kneel before it sprang?
Because it was preying.

What did the Mammoth think of the grape's home?
De-vine.

My dad is so short-sighted he can't get to sleep unless he counts dinosaurs.

What goes "Munch, munch, ouch!" when eating food?
A dinosaur with a bad tooth.

Did a Diplodocus catch a head cold after getting its feet wet?
Yes, but not until two weeks later.

Why are a coin and a dinosaur alike?
The both have a head and a tail.

What did the baby porcupine say when he backed into a cactus?
Is that you, Mum?

What do you get if you cross a sabre-toothed tiger with an elderly gentleman in a red coat and white beard?
Santa Claws.

Why should you not grab a dinosaur by his tail?
It may be his tail but it could be your end.

Who were the snootiest dinosaurs?
The ones that lived in trees, they looked down
on all the other dinosaurs.

Is anyone safe when a man-eating sabre-
toothed tiger is on the loose?
Yes – women and children.

Did you hear about the Tyrannosaurus whose
teeth were so bad he knocked one out every
time he poked out his tongue?

Caveman: Tomorrow your mother is going to make a Brachiosaurus pie. Who is going to eat it?

Eldest Son: I will.

Caveman: Good. And tomorrow I am going to pick some apples. Who will eat them?

Eldest Son: I will.

Caveman: Great! And also tomorrow I am going to hunt for Tyrannosaurus. Who will come with me?

Eldest Son: I've volunteered for everything so far. I think it is someone else's turn.

What's the difference between an Archaeopteryx with two wings and an Archaeopteryx with one wing?
Only a difference of a pinion.

Did you hear about the Ichthyosaurus that went deaf?
His friends bought him a herring aid.

Caveman: Did you hear a loud noise this morning?
Cavewoman: Yes, what was it – the crack of dawn?
Caveman: No, the break of day.

Caveman: What can I do with my old bowling balls?
Cavewoman: Give 'em to the Mammoths to play marbles with.

What was the favourite take-away meal in prehistoric times?
Kentucky fried Archaeopteryx.

What happened when the male Triceratops met the female Triceratops?
It was love at first fright.

Cavewoman: I think I heard a dinosaur coming into our cave. Are you awake?
Caveman: No.

First Palaeontologist: When I was in Africa I hunted dinosaurs on horseback.
Second Palaeontologist: Well, I never, I didn't know dinosaurs rode horses.

Thomas: I've got a new pet dinosaur.
Daniel: Where are you going to keep it?
Thomas: In my bedroom.
Daniel: But what about the smell?
Thomas: Oh, he'll soon get used to that.

What happened to the dinosaurs when they ate a comedian?
They had a feast of fun.

A herd of twelve Mammoths fell over cliff and all but four died. How many were left?
Four, of course!

A boy was walking his pet dinosaur through the park when a policeman approached.
"Do you have a licence for that?" asked the policeman.
"Don't be silly," the boy replied, "He's not old enough to drive."

What happened when the dinosaur chewed a bone for an hour?
When he got up he only had three legs.

What do you get if you cross a dinosaur with spiked shoes?
A very cross dinosaur.

What is worse than a Diplodocus with a stiff neck?
A Mammoth with a stuffed-up nose.

First Triceratops: My, hasn't your little girl grown!
Second Triceratops: Yes, she's certainly gruesome.

What did the Iguanodon say when he saw Snow White and the seven dwarfs?
"Oh, good. An eight-course meal."

Knock, knock.
Who's there?
Ivan.
Ivan who?
Ivan Allosaurus with me.

What did the Arctic Mammoth have for lunch?
Iceburgers.

How do you run over a Mammoth?
Climb up its tail, dash to its head and slide
down its trunk.

What had three wings, three eyes and
two bills?
An Archaeopteryx with spare parts.

What's the difference between a sick dinosaur
and a dead bee?
One's a seedy beast and the other's a
bee deceased.

How do you make a Mammoth laugh?
Tickle its ivories.

Caveman: Our dog is a wonderful watchdog. No one and nothing ever gets anywhere near our cave without us knowing.
Friend: Does he growl and bark and howl?
Caveman: No, he crawls into bed with us.

When a baby dinosaur cries in the night who gets up?
The whole neighbourhood.

What do you call a Diplodocus that stands on your toe?
Anything you like – his ears are too far away to hear you.

What did the palaeontologist use to cut up the enormous fossil of a Triceratops?
A dino-saw.

What carries hundreds of needles but never sews?
A porcupine.

What's grey, and lumpy and weighs eight tons?
A dinosaur with mumps.

First Mammoth: I hear that egg shampoo is
good for your hair.
Second Mammoth: But how do you get an
Archaeopteryx to lay an egg on your head?

What prehistoric creature lived on the beach?
A dino-shore.

How did the Diplodocus prevent a head cold
moving down to his chest?
He tied a knot in his neck.

What do you call the strongest
Archaeopteryx?
A featherweight champion.

What aftershave did dinosaurs wear?
Brute.

Why did the dinosaur chase its tail?
To make both ends meet.

Stegosaurus: Ask me if I'm a Stegosaurus.
Tyrannosaurus: Are you a Stegosaurus?
Stegosaurus: Yes, I am. Now ask me if I'm a Archaeopteryx.
Tyrannosaurus: Are you an Archaeopteryx?
Stegosaurus: How can you be so stupid? Didn't I just tell you I'm a Stegosaurus?

What can a dinosaur swallow that can also swallow a dinosaur?
Water.

What time was it when the dinosaur ate
the Prime Minister?
Ate p.m.

What is smaller than a dinosaur's mouth?
Anything it eats.

First Dinosaur Hunter: Once I was in real
danger. I was surrounded by wild animals.
Second Dinosaur Hunter: How did you escape?
First Dinosaur Hunter: I got off the merry-go-
round.

When is it good for a dinosaur to lose
its temper?
When it has a bad one.

Caveman: I can lift a Stegosaurus with
one hand.
Cavewoman: I bet you can't.
Caveman: You find me a Stegosaurus with one
hand and I'll lift it.

First Triceratops: My husband says I'm the
most beautiful dinosaur in the world.
Second Triceratops: Yes, my husband's got bad
eyesight too.

Why didn't the Mammoths go in Noah's Ark?
They were too busy packing their trunks.

How long were the legs of a Stegosaurus?
Long enough to reach the ground.

What would you get if you crossed a pigeon,
a frog and a prehistoric animal?
A pigeon-toad dinosaur.

Stegosaurus: I have a terrible pain in my stomach.

Tyrannosaurus: What have you been eating?

Stegosaurus: Well, I did have a Franciscan monk yesterday.

Tyrannosaurus: How did you cook him?

Stegosaurus: I boiled him.

Tyrannosaurus: Ah, that's what's caused your discomfort. Franciscans should not be boiled – they're friars.

What do you call a baby dinosaur that bites?
A pain in the knee.

What would you get if you crossed a watchdog
with a dinosaur?
Very nervous postmen.

First Palaeontologist: Why do you carry a
compass with you when you go fossil hunting?
Second Palaeontologist: So I know whether I'm
coming or going.

First Mammoth: Where do fleas go in the winter?
Second Mammoth: Search me!

What happened to the dinosaur who ate a sheep?
He felt baaaaad.

What do you get if a dinosaur sits on your piano?
A flat note.

What do you get if you cross an
Archaeopteryx with a cement mixer?
A layer of concrete.

What do you call a caveman who puts his right
arm down a dinosaur's throat?
Lefty.

What do you get if you cross a Diplodocus with
a rooster?
A creature that wakes people who live on the
top floor.

Why did the dinosaur scratch himself?
Because he was the only one who knew where
he itched.

Who gets fed up with people?
A man-eating dinosaur.

What were dinosaur skins used for?
Holding the dinosaur together.

How do you get a Diplodocus into a matchbox?
Take the matches out first.

Knock, knock.
Who's there?
Ivor.
Ivor who?
Ivor you let me in or I'll set my pet Iguanodon on you.

What happens when a Tyrannosaurus swallows
a bunch of keys?
He gets lockjaw.

How do you address a dinosaur?
Very carefully.

When the caveman put his hand in the
dinosaur's mouth to see how many teeth it had,
what did the dinosaur do?
Closed its mouth to see how many fingers the
caveman had.

What is as big as Tyrannosaurus rex but
doesn't weigh anything?
His shadow.

Why is a dinosaur's nose in the middle
of its face?
Because it's the scenter.

What do you call the nose of a
deceased dinosaur?
The dead scenter.

What do you get if you cross a hyena with a sabre-toothed tiger?
I don't know, but if he laughs you'd better join in.

Why was the Brontosaurus wrinkled?
It ate a lot of prunes.

Did you hear about the dinosaur that sat up all night wondering where the sun had gone?
Next day it dawned on him.

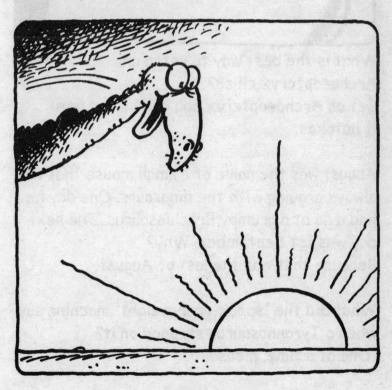

What is the best way to catch an
Archaeopteryx chick?
Get an Archaeopteryx egg and hold it until
it hatches.

August was the name of a small mouse that was
always arguing with the dinosaurs. One day he
had a go at a grumpy Brachiosaurus. The next
day was 1st September. Why?
Because that was the last of August.

What did the "speak-your-weight" machine say
when a Tyrannosaurus stepped on it?
"One at a time, please."

What happened when the sabre-toothed tiger swallowed a coin?
There was money in the kitty.

Young Mammoth: Mum, all my friends say I'm ugly.
Mother Mammoth: Don't take any notice, just comb your face and go out to play.

Bill: What's the difference between a dinosaur and a pillar box?
Jill: I don't know.
Bill: Well, I'm certainly not going to send you out with my post!

Two cavemen met in the jungle and one of them had a strange-looking bird with him. "What sort of bird is that?" asked one of the cavemen.

"It's a gobble-it bird," said the other. "It will eat anything you say. Just watch. Gobble-it bird, bananas." The bird flew across the clearing and devoured all the bananas in sight. "Gobble-it bird, my spear." said the caveman and the bird devoured it in an instant.

"I'd like that bird." said the first caveman and they agreed upon a sale.

The caveman took the bird back to his cave and his wife said "What on earth is that?"

"It's a gobble-it bird," said the caveman "It will eat anything you say."

"Gobble-it bird?" said the incredulous wife. "Gobble-it bird, my foot!"

Female Dinosaur: Will you love me when I'm old and ugly?
Male Dinosaur: Of course I do.

What do you get if you cross a Diplodocus with a hedgehog?
A very long toothbrush.

How do you make a dinosaur float?
Take two scoops of ice cream, a glass of lemonade and add one dinosaur.

What do you get if you cross a Mammoth with a kangaroo?
Large holes all over Australia.

Some dinosaurs were walking through the jungle. There was a dinosaur in front of a dinosaur, a dinosaur behind two dinosaurs and a dinosaur between two dinosaurs. How many dinosaurs were there?
Three dinosaurs walking in a line.

What does a sabre-toothed tiger rest it
head on?
A caterpillow.

Why did the Mammoth cross the road?
To make a trunk call.

Where did a Brachiosaurus sleep?
Anywhere it wanted to.

What do you call a prehistoric creature that
gets runs in cricket?
A dino-score.

Which prehistoric animal liked to play hide and seek?
A dino-saw-ya.

What's the difference between a dinosaur and peanut butter?
A dinosaur doesn't stick to the roof of your mouth.

Doctor, doctor! I think I'm a sabre-toothed tiger.
How long have you felt like this?
Ever since I was a cub.

What do dinosaurs sing at Christmas?
Jungle bells, jungle bells.

What do you get if you cross a Mammoth with a computer?
A 5-ton know-it-all.

What do you call the female prehistoric creature that married a Red Indian?
A dino-squaw.

What happened when the dinosaur ate a stick of dynamite?
He blew his cool.

Why did the Mammoth have a fur coat?
Because he looked silly in a plastic mac.

What do you get if you cross a sabre-toothed
tiger with a duck?
A duck-filled-fatty-puss.

What's the best way to avoid getting infected
by biting dinosaurs?
Don't bite any.

Why did the dinosaur lie on his back?
To trip up low-flying aircraft.

What would you call a Mammoth that muttered to himself?
A mumbo jumbo.

What has four legs and flies?
A dead dinosaur.

What do you get if you cross a witch
with a dinosaur?
A crazy animal that chases aeroplanes.

Why did the Triceratops give up boxing?
He didn't want to spoil his looks.

What did the policeman say to the Iguanodon
when they met?
Keep away from my dog – I don't want him to
bite you, he's the only dog I've got.

Cavewoman: You feet are sticking out of the bedclothes.
Caveman: I know.
Cavewoman: Aren't they cold?
Caveman: They're freezing.
Cavewoman: Well, why don't you pull them in?
Caveman: What! No way am I going to have those cold things in bed with me!

Why do man-eating dinosaurs like transport cafés?
Because they serve a wide variety of drivers.

Caveman: What's warm and tasty, comes from the jungle and is found in your kitchen?
Cavewoman: I don't know, what is warm and tasty, comes from the jungle and is found in my kitchen?
Caveman: Snake and pigmy pie.

Where would you find an Allosaurus?
Wherever you left him.

What do you get if you dance with a dinosaur?
Flat feet.

What did one dinosaur say to the other?
"Who was that lady I saw you with last night?"
"That was no lady. That was my dinner."

What prehistoric reptile went down the yellow brick road?
The Lizard of Oz.

Caveboy: Dad, why does the ocean roar?
Caveman: You'd roar, too if you had crabs in your bed!

A man went into a police station with a dinosaur on a lead. "What should I do with this?" he asked.

"Take it to Jurassic Park." said the policeman. The following day the policemen saw the man and he had the dinosaur with him. "I told you to take that to Jurassic Park," said the policeman.

"I did," said the man. "And now I'm taking him to the pictures."

Where would you see dog-like dinosaurs?
Jurassic Bark.

What did the hotel manager say to the
Mammoth who couldn't pay his bill?
Pack your trunk and clear off.

Why didn't the Stegosaurus cross the road?
He didn't want to be mistaken for a chicken.

* NAUGHTY DINO WORDS.

What prehistoric creature was known for its
bad language?
The dino-swore.

Who would win a boxing match between a
dinosaur and a porcupine?
The porcupine – on points.

What do you get if you cross a hyena with a
sabre-toothed tiger?
A gigglepuss.

What do you get if you cross a Tyrannosaurus with a lamb?
You have to get a new lamb.

Why couldn't the two Mammoths go swimming?
Because they only had one pair of trunks between them.

What do you get if you cross a pig with a dinosaur?
Jurassic Pork.

Why did dinosaurs never forget?
No one ever told them anything.

How do you make a dinosaur sandwich?
First, you get a very large loaf . . .

Two dinosaurs were arguing. "I didn't come here to be insulted," yelled the first dinosaur. "Really?" said the other dinosaur. "Where do you usually go?"

Which dinosaur could jump higher than a tree?
All of them. Trees can't jump.

How do you stop a dirty dinosaur from smelling?
Cut off his nose.

How do you know you have a Mammoth in bed with you?
By the letter M embroidered on his pyjamas.

What do you need to know to teach a dinosaur?
More than the dinosaur.

Did you hear about the man-eating dinosaur
that had a bad stomach?
He ate someone that disagreed with him.

Why did Mammoths have trunks?
Because glove compartments hadn't been
invented.

What does a Plesiosaur pick its nose with?
Ichthyosaurus fingers.

What does a Mammoth do when he breaks
a toe?
He calls a tow truck.

Did you hear about the palaeontologist who
does dinosaur impressions?
He does the smells.

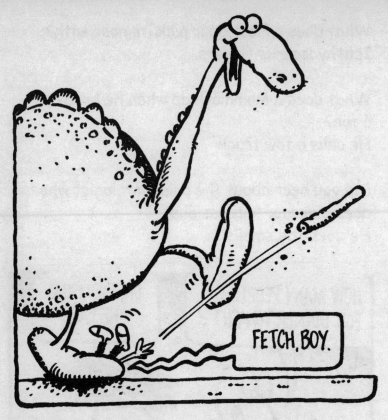

How do you stop a dinosaur attacking you?
Throw a stick and shout, "Fetch, boy."

Where was the dinosaur when the sun
went down?
In the dark.

Why did the Archaeopteryx put his leg in his
mouth in the restaurant?
Because he wanted to foot the bill.

Teacher: And this prehistoric creature was called a Brachiosaurus.
Pupil: Sir, why was it called a Brachiosaurus?
Teacher: Because it looks like a Brachiosaurus, that's why!

Why were three dinosaurs trying to get into a phone box?
They wanted to play squash.

What do you call a fossil that doesn't want to work?
Lazy bones.

A Brachiosaurus fell over a cliff and all his
mates gathered round to see how he was.
One of them said, "Did the fall hurt you?"
"Oh, no," he said "The fall was OK, it was the
sudden stop that hurt."

What do you call being frightened of sabre-toothed tigers?
Clawstrophobia.

What do you call being frightened of sabre-toothed tigers?
Sensible.

What do you do with a green dinosaur?
Wait until it ripens.

What happened to Ray when a Mammoth stepped on him?
He became an X-Ray.

How much did the psychiatrist charge the Brachiosaurus?
£100 for the consultation and £600 for the couch.

A man was walking down the street with a dinosaur on a lead.
Another man came along and said, "Where did you get him?"
"I won him at the fair," replied the dinosaur.

What do you get when dinosaurs crash
their cars?
Tyrannosaurus wrecks.

Why doesn't the Triceratops ride
a motorbike?
His horns won't fit in the crash helmet.

What was the Diplodocus's favourite ballet?
Swamp Lake.

What do you get if you cross a Diplodocus with
a racehorse?
An animal that is very hard to ride, but great
in a photofinish.

Dad! I have just found a fossilised dinosaur!
So what, I've been married to one for years.

What does a polite man-eating dinosaur say?
Pleased to eat you.

What dinosaur never gives up?
A Try-try-try-ceratops.

Why did the Tyrannosaurus have such
sharp teeth?
To open tins of fruit.

Seen in a palaeontologist's bookcase:
Wild Tyrannosaurus by Claudia Armoff.

What dinosaur could you ride in a rodeo?
A Bronco-saurus.

What did the Tyrannosaurus say to
the caveman?
It's been nice gnawing you.

Bill: I've got a new pet. It's a dinosaur. Would
you like to come and play with it?
Jill: Does it bite?
Bill: That's what I want to find out.

What type of baby would thrive on
Stegosaurus milk?
A baby Stegosaurus.

Cavewoman: You look bright and breezy
this morning.
Caveman: Yes, that's because last night I had
a double rest.
Cavewoman: What do you mean?
Caveman: I dreamt I was sleeping.

Why did the Triceratops buy a hammer?
To burst his pimples.

What prehistoric creature talks, and talks,
and talks, and talks?
A dino-bore.

What is the Diplodocus's favourite sweet?
Marsh-mallow.

Why did the dinosaur's car stop?
It had a flat Tire-annosaurus.

How do you stop a herd of Mammoths charging
at you?
Make a trunk call and reverse the charge.

Andy: An Allosaurus wanted to cross a river to get to his friends on the other side, but the river was too deep to wade through and too fast to swim through. How did he get across?
Sandie: I give up.
Andy: So did the Allosaurus.

What do you call a sabre-toothed tiger killing its prey?
A cat-e-gory.

What tool was used by a reptile carpenter?
A dino-saw.

What do Triceratops sit on?
Tricerabottoms.

What do you call a sabre-toothed
tiger's movement?
A cat-walk.

What do you call a sabre-toothed tiger on a
tree branch?
A cat-a-logue.

I've got an Ichthyosaurus.
Where do you keep it?
In the bath.
What do you do if you want to have a bath?
I blindfold it.

I've got an Ichthyosaurus.
I suggest you go to the hospital and have
it treated.

What has four legs like a dinosaur, a head
like a dinosaur and a tail like a dinosaur, but
isn't a dinosaur?
A picture of a dinosaur.

What's the difference between a dinosaur
and a doughnut?
You can't dunk a dinosaur in your tea.

What prehistoric creature made the best
clothes?
A dino-sewer.

What prehistoric animal could fly?
A dino-soar.

Why are there old bones in museums?
They can't afford new ones.

Girl Triceratops: Would you say I'm pretty?
Boy Triceratops: No.
Girl Triceratops: Would you say I'm ugly?
Boy Triceratops: No.
Girl Triceratops: Well, what would you say?
Boy Triceratops: I'd say you were pretty ugly.
Girl Triceratops: Ooh, thank you!

Aunty Gladys went into a pet shop to buy a present for her nephew. The pet owner offered her a dinosaur.

"Are you sure this will make a good pet?' she asked.

"Of course, madam," said the shop owner "He'll eat anything and he's especially fond of children."

Why did the Brachiosaurus wag its tail?
Because no one else would wag it for him.

Which dinosaur wrote Wuthering Heights?
Emily Bronte-saurus.

Where would you see a prehistoric cow?
In a moo-seum.

Seen in a palaeontologist's bookcase:
Dinosaurs' Eating Habits by Nora Bone.

Did you hear about the caveman with
pedestrian eyes?
They looked both ways before they crossed.

A Brachiosaurus and the son of a Brachiosaurus were walking through the jungle. The young Brachiosaurus was the son of the older Brachiosaurus but the older Brachiosaurus was not the younger one's father. Who was the older creature?
His mother.

Nicky: I wish I had enough money to buy a dinosaur.
Ricky: What would you do with a dinosaur?
Nicky: I don't want one, I just wish I had that much money.

Which prehistoric creatures made the
best police?
Tricera-cops.

What do you call a prehistoric bird?
A Jurassic lark.

Seen in a palaeontologist's bookcase:
Making Outsize Clothes by Ma Moth.

What happened when the Triceratops went to
a party?
Everyone hung their coats on his horns.

What's an alligator's favourite game?
Snap!

What is large and grey and can see just as well from either end?
A dinosaur with his eyes shut.

Teacher: Can you tell me the difference between a Mammoth and a bison?
Jimmy: Yes, sir. You can't wash your hands in a Mammoth.

What do man-eating dinosaurs like for lunch?
Baked beings on toast.

Why did the Diplodocus devour a factory.
Because he was a plant eater.

What was the Iguanodon after gardening?
Dino-sore.

What's the best way to speak to a
Tyrannosaurus?
Long distance.

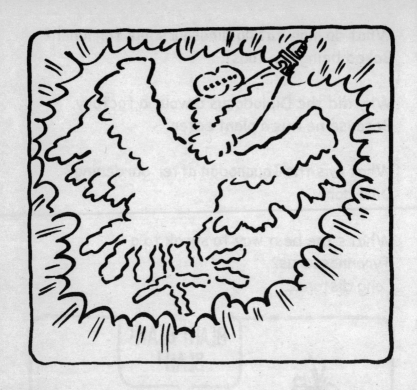

Why did the Archaeopteryx stick its beak into the light socket?
To get an electric bill.

What did the Tyrannosaurus say when he saw a caveman asleep in a hammock?
Ah, breakfast in bed!

Why did the Diplodocus take a tape measure to bed?
He wanted to see how long he slept.

What prehistoric ships are found under
the sea?
Tyrannosaurus wrecks.

What's worse than a Mammoth with a
sore nose?
A giant tortoise with claustrophobia.

What do you get if you cross a Mammoth with
a mouse?
A trunkful of cheese.

Why did the Archaeopteryx watch the
council worker?
He had heard that the man was going to lay a
pavement and he wanted to see how it was
done.

What is a Brachiosaurus's favourite
playground toy?
A dino-see-saw.

First Caveman: We had roast boar for dinner yesterday.
Second Caveman: Wild?
First Caveman: Well, he wasn't too pleased about it.

What do you get if you cross a tin of plasters with a baby sabre-toothed tiger?
A first aid kit.

How can you stop a dinosaur from charging?
Take away his credit card.

What do you give a dinosaur that's
feeling sick?
Plenty of room.

What did the Tyrannosaurus say after he'd
eaten a clown?
I've got a funny feeling.

Seen in a palaeontologist's bookcase:
Hunting for Dinosaurs by Hugo Furst.

Did you hear about the scientist who crossed a parrot with a Tyrannosaurus?
He got a creature that bit off his arm and then said, "Who's a pretty boy, then?"

Seen in a palaeontologist's bookcase:
Flying Dinosaurs by Terry Dactill.

What happened to the Stegosaurus that swallowed a light bulb?
He spat it out and was delighted!
Why did he eat the light bulb in the first place?
He fancied a light snack.

Did the dinosaur take a bath?
Why, is there one missing?

Which dinosaur had the highest intelligence?
Diplodocus.

What happened to the Mammoth in a brewery?
He got trunk.

Would you rather a Tyrannosaurus attacked you, or a Triceratops?
I'd prefer the Tyrannosaurus to attack the Triceratops.

What do you get if you cross a dinosaur with a kangaroo?
Tricera-hops.

Did you know that Brachiosaurus, was 25 metres long and 16 metres high and it slept in a bed it made itself?
Sounds like a lot of bunk.

What do you get if you cross a Mammoth with a parasol?
An umbrellaphant.

Mr Tyrannosaurus: I've brought a friend home for dinner.
Mrs Tyrannosaurus: Lovely dear. Just put him in the freezer. We'll have him next week.

Did you hear about the Brontosaurus who ate
all the apples on a tree?
It died of apple-plexy.

How did a baby dinosaur fit into an egg?
Eggsactly.

A man walked into a pub and asked, "Do you
serve Australians?"
"Yes, certainly, sir," said the landlord.
"Good, I'll have a pint a beer and two
Australians for my pet dinosaur."

Two cavemen were out hunting dinosaurs.
Suddenly a small dinosaur leapt from the
undergrowth and bit off one caveman's leg.
"A small dinosaur has just bitten off my leg."
yelled the caveman.
"Which one?" asked his companion.
"I don't know," yelled the first. "All small
dinosaurs look the same to me."

What prehistoric creature ate his
mother's sister?
An aunt-eater.

What's the difference between a flea-ridden dinosaur and a bored guest?
One is going to itch, the other is itching to go.

A Stegosaurus walked into a bar and ordered a gin and tonic with two slices of lemon. The Stegosaurus took the drink to a corner table and sipped it quietly.
A customer at the bar said, "Now there's something you don't see very often."
The barman said, "You're right. Most customers have only one slice of lemon."

Did you hear about the dinosaur who fell in love with a piano?
He admired her lovely teeth.

Seen in a palaeontologist's bookcase:
Running from a Sabre-Toothed Tiger by
Claude Bottom.

Why did the Mammoth chew camphor balls?
To keep moths out of his trunk.

What do you call a dinosaur after it is one year old?
A two-year-old dinosaur.

An Allosaurus was walking through the jungle when he saw a fairy. "Allo," he said. "I've never seen a fairy before. What's your name?"
"Allo Allosaurus. My name is Nuff," said the fairy.
"That's an unusual name." said the Allosaurus.
"No it's not," said the fairy indignantly. "Have you never heard of Fairy Nuff?"

What do you do if a dinosaur comes to your picnic?
Offer him the biggest sandwich.

Seen in a palaeontologist's bookcase:
Large Birds by Albert Ross.

Why did the Diplodocus never get fat?
Because it ate necks to nothing.

What's big and ugly and red in the face?
A dinosaur holding its breath.

What's big and ugly and bright red all over?
An embarrassed dinosaur.

What did the sabre-toothed tiger who had no
money say?
I'm paw.

How did dinosaurs pass exams?
With extinction.

What time is it when a dinosaur sits on
your fence?
Time to get a new fence.

Have you ever seen a man-eating dinosaur?
No, but in the café this morning I saw a man
eating chicken!

What does a sabre-toothed tiger use to
smooth its fur?
A cat-a-comb.

As a ship anchored off a desert island two dinosaurs were watching from the undergrowth. Some of the crew lowered a boat and began rowing to the shore.

"We'd better get away from here, fast," said one dinosaur.

"Why?" asked the other. "They look friendly enough."

"That may be so," said the first dinosaur. "But we're supposed to be extinct."

Why should you feel sorry for an Archaeopteryx?
Because he always has a bill facing him.

What's the best way to get out from under
a Tyrannosaurus?
Wait until he moves away.

Boy: What is extinct?
Father: Well, if all life on earth was wiped out,
you could say the human race is extinct.
Boy: But to whom would I say it?

A caveman walking through the jungle fainted when he saw a Tyrannosaurus approaching. When he came to the Tyrannosaurus appeared to be praying. "Thank you for not eating me," said the caveman.
"Be quiet," said the Tyrannosaurus. "I'm saying grace."

A Brachiosaurus walked up to a dazed friend who had just run headlong into a tree.
"Have an accident?" he asked.
"No thanks," said the injured animal. "I've just had one."

Why couldn't the Mammoth travel on the inter-city train?
His trunk wouldn't fit under the seat.

What do dinosaurs have that no other animal has?
Baby dinosaurs, of course!

Seen in a palaeontologist's bookcase:
Prehistoric Animals by Dinah Soar.

Why was Brontosaurus a bad dancer?
Because he had two left feet.

What did the grape say when the dinosaur
trod on it?
Nothing, it just let out a little wine.

A policeman knocked on a woman's front door,
but as she wouldn't come to the door he
shouted through the letter box, "Madam, your
husband has been flattened by a dinosaur."
The woman replied, "I'm in the bath – just slip
him under the door."

Why did the dinosaur run fast over the box of corn flakes?
Because it said "Tear along the dotted line".

What's the difference between a lame dinosaur and a lumberjack?
One hops and chews, the other chops and hews.

What's the scariest dinosaur in the world?
The terror-dactyl.

Why did dinosaurs eat raw meat?
They didn't know how to cook.

There were four large dinosaurs standing under a tree but none of them got wet. Why was that?
It wasn't raining.

What lies on the ground four feet in the air?
A dead dinosaur.

Did you hear about the man-eating dinosaur
that went on a luxury cruise?
At dinner on the first night he did not want to
see the menu, he asked for the passenger list.

Seen in a palaeontologist's bookcase:
The Art of Necking by Dee Plidocus.

What is the last hair on a dinosaur's tail called?
A dinosaur hair.

What does a Mammoth do if he breaks a toe?
Gives up ballet dancing.

Two cavemen were out in the jungle when they came across some large dinosaur tracks.
"Right, said the first, "you see where they go and I'll check where they come from."

What do you get if you cross a Tyrannosaurus
with a computer?
Mega-bytes.

Caveman: What's a good way of putting
on weight?
Cavewoman: Eat a peach, swallow the centre –
and you've gained a stone.

Did you hear about the dinosaur that saw a
sign that said "Wet Paint" – so he did!

As the two cave men emerged from their cave they were greeted by an enormous dinosaur and all they had to defend themselves were two small sticks.
The first cave man said: "You go and attack him and I'll keep you covered."

What do you get if you cross a mouse with an Allosaurus?
A world cheese shortage.

What was the first thing the Tyrannosaurus
ate when he got his new false teeth?
The dentist.

Triceratops: I went to the beauty parlour
yesterday. I was there for over two hours.
Tyrannosaurus: What did you have done?
Triceratops: Nothing, I just went in for
an estimate.

What should you do if a Tyrannosaurus
borrows your comic?
Wait for him to give it back.

Why did the baby dinosaur stop having
baby food?
He wanted something to get his teeth into.

What does an absent-minded
Archaeopteryx do?
She often mislays her eggs.

Brachiosaurus: Quick, someone help me – a Mammoth has fallen into the mud right up to his toes.
Stegosaurus: Up to his toes? Why doesn't he just walk out, then?
Brachiosaurus: He fell in upside down!

What do you call a dead dinosaur?
Nothing, he can't hear you.

What do you get if you cross a Tyrannosaurus with a cow?
A creature that eats anyone who tries to milk it.

What did the mouse say when a Tyrannosaurus asked to borrow some money?
Sorry, I'm a bit short.

What do you get if you cross a dog with a Diplodocus?
A creature that barks at low-flying aeroplanes.

The dinosaurs in Jurassic Park held a football match. It was a good game and towards the end the score was six all. One of the best players was a tiny ant who had superb ball control. With only two minutes to the end of the game he gained possession of the ball, went scuttling down the field and was just about to score when the Tyrannosaurus, who was on the opposing side, trod on him and squashed him flat.

The Archaeopteryx, who was refereering the game, ordered Tyrannosaurus off the pitch.

"It was an accident," Tyrannosaurus pleaded. "I didn't mean to kill the ant. I just tried to trip him up."

Fred: How do you make a statue of a dinosaur?
Sculptor: You get a large stone and cut away
anything that doesn't look like a dinosaur.

Caveboy: My dad's so tough he can kill an
Iguanodon with his bare hands.
Cavegirl: So what, my dad's so tough it took
five hours in the microwave to cook him.

What do you get if you cross a dinosaur
with a wizard?
Tyrannosaurus hex.

What's the difference between a
Brontosaurus and a Matterbaby?
What's a Matterbaby?
Nothing's the matter, but thanks for asking.

On which side does a Mammoth have the
most hair?
On the outside.

Did you hear about the creature who did not eat breakfast, tea or supper?
He was a dinner-saurus.

First Palaeontologist: If you were in the jungle and a dinosaur charged you, what would you do?
Second Palaeontologist: Pay him.

What do you do with a blue dinosaur?
Try to cheer it up.

TUESDAY

When do dinosaurs eat you?
Chewsday.

Teacher: Your essay about a dinosaur is the same as your friend's.
Pupil: Yes, it's the same dinosaur.

How many legs did Triceratops have?
Six – fore-legs in front and two legs behind.

When does a Tyrannosaurus bite you?
Winceday.

When does an Allosuarus cook you?
Fried-day.

What do you get if you cross a sabre-toothed tiger with a dog?
An animal that eats people and then buries the bones.

Young Willie went to the Natural History Museum with his class to see the dinosaur skeletons. When he got home his mother asked if he enjoyed it. "Oh yes," he said, "I've never been to a dead zoo before."

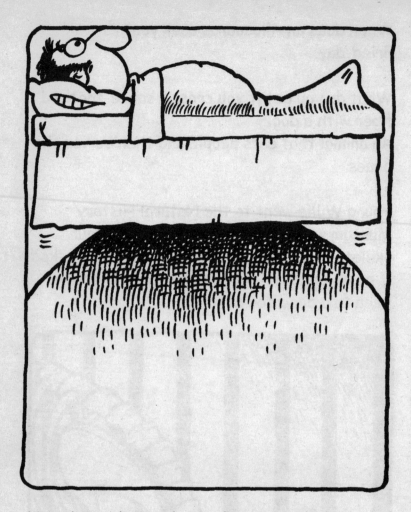

How do you know when a dinosaur is hiding
under your bed?
Your nose is pressed against the ceiling.

Why weren't Mammoths allowed on the beach?
In case their trunks fell down.

Teacher: What can you tell me about
the dinosaurs?
Pupil: They're all dead.

What do you call a dinosaur in a phone box?
Stuck.

What goes ha, ha, ha, plop?
A dinosaur laughing his head off.
What do you get if you cross a worm
with a dinosaur?
Great big holes in your garden.

How does a dinosaur make toast?
He puts it under the gorilla.

Who finished first in the Diplodocus race?
It was a dead heat – they finished neck
and neck.

Mrs Triceratops: My new baby is the image of
his father.
Miss Triceratops: Never mind, at least
he's healthy.

How did a dinosaur try to impress people?
By putting his beast foot forward.

A dinosaur went into a bar and ordered a glass
of orange juice. £2, please," said the barman.
As the dinosaur drank his orange the barman
said, "We don't get many dinosaurs in here."
"I'm not surprised," said the dinosaur, "with
orange juice at £2 a glass."

What do you get if you cross a dinosaur
skeleton with a clock?
A rattling good time.

What's an Ichthyosaurus's favourite
Indian meal?
Fin-da-loo.

What is the Diplodocus's favourite
breakfast cereal?
Ready Neck.

Why did the Iguanodon wear sunglasses
on holiday?
He didn't want to be recognised.

Did you hear about the unlucky dinosaur who
picked some bananas?
They were empty.

Patient: I keep seeing dinosaurs.
Doctor: Have you seen a psychiatrist?
Patient: No, just dinosaurs.

How do you address a dinosaur?
Very carefully.

What do you get on your bottom if you sit in a restaurant for too long?
A diner-sore.

Why does a Mammoth have a trunk?
It's something to hide in when he sees a mouse.

142

Two dinosaurs fell over a cliff.
Boom, boom!

What do you give a Mammoth who
is exhausted?
Trunkquillisers.

Diplodocus was not very good at apologising –
it always took him a long time to swallow
his pride.

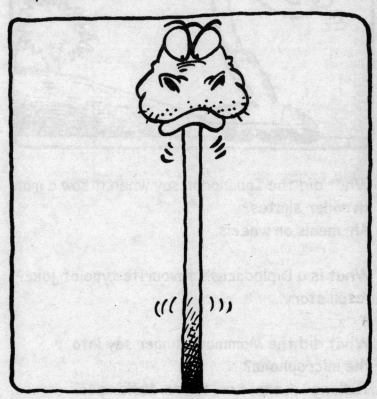

What did the Iguanodon say when it saw a man
on roller skates?
Ah, meals on wheels.

What is a Diplodocus's favourite type of joke?
A tall story.

What did the Mammoth singer say into
the microphone?
Tusking . . . one, two, three, tusking.

What happened to Batman and Robin when a dinosaur trod on them?
They became Flatman and Ribbon.

How did the Mammoth get into the phone box?
He ran round and round until he was all in.

Why was the Tyrannosaurus musical?
He had sharp teeth.

Why did the lady Mammoth put her hair in rollers before going to bed?
She wanted to wake curly next morning.

What dinosaur was made of stone?
Tyrannosaurus rocks.

Two dinosaurs were walking along the promenade at Blackpool.
One said to the other: "It's quiet for a bank holiday."

On his way to Jurassic Park a Tyrannosaurus met two Brachiosauruses each with an Archaeopteryx on its back, a Diplodocus with a crab hanging on its tail, and a Triceratops with a bird perched on one of its horns. How many creatures were going to Jurassic Park?
Only one, the Tyrannosaurus. All the rest were going in the opposite direction.

Did you hear about the lazy dinosaur?
He waited for another dinosaur to roar and then just nodded his head.

Teacher: Some dates are written with the
letters AD after them. What do the letters
AD mean?
Pupil: After Dinosaurs.

Boy Brachiosaurus to girl Brachiosaurus: One
day we shall have children of our own and we'll
hear the thunder of tiny feet.

What's the best way to raise a Brachiosaurus?
Use a crane.

Who lost a herd of Mammoths?
Big Bo Peep.

Who won the dinosaur beauty contest?
No one.

How many dinosaurs can you get into an empty sports stadium?
Only one, after that it's not empty.

What tartan did dinosaurs wear?
Tyrannosaurus checks.

What's the difference between a clap of
thunder and a dinosaur with toothache?
One may cause it to pour with rain, the other
may cause it to roar with pain.

First Palaeontologist: If a dinosaur's head is pointing towards the north where would its tail be pointing?
Second Palaeontologist: To the south.
First Palaeontologist: No, to the ground.

Where did Mammoths go on holiday?
Tuscany.

What did the banana do when it saw a dinosaur?
The banana split.

Where did dinosaurs buy their clothes?
At jungle sales.

What do you give a Mammoth that
has collapsed?
Trunk-to-trunk resuscitation.

Doctor, doctor! I keep having these terrible
dreams. I keep dreaming that my bedroom
is full of dinosaurs playing chess, what
should I do?
Hide the chess set.

What do you get if you cross an Ichthyosaurus
with a Mammoth?
Swimming trunks.

What lies on its back four feet up in the air?
A drunk dinosaur.

How do you stop a dinosaur howling in the back
of a car?
Put him in the front.

What's the difference between a fly and an Archaeopteryx?
An Archaeopteryx could fly but a fly can't Archaeopteryx.

Why did the Mammoth drink two litres of antifreeze?
So he wouldn't have to grow a winter coat.

What dinosaur was black, could fly and cawed?
Tyrannosaurus rooks.

Triceratops: I've just come back from the beauty parlour.
Tyrannosaurus: Pity it was closed!

How do you know that a dinosaur has been in your fridge?
By the footprints in the butter.

Where did the dinosaurs go for dinner?
To a beastro.

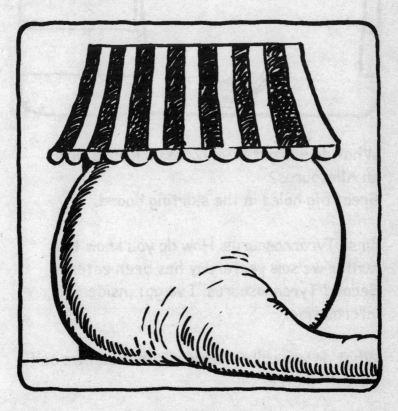

What do you get if you cross a mouse with
an Allosaurus?
Great big holes in the skirting board.

First Tyrannosaurus: How do you know that
hunter we saw yesterday has been eaten?
Second Tyrannosaurus: I've got inside
information.

What do you call a Mammoth that lost its calf?
De-calf-inated.

Mother sabre-toothed tiger: What are you cubs doing?

Young sabre-toothed tiger: We're chasing a hunter around a tree.

Mother sabre-toothed tiger: How many times have I told you not to play with your food?

What did Mrs Tyrannosaurus say to her son at supper?

It's rude to talk with someone in your mouth.

What branch of the armed forces did the
Mammoth join?
The Hair Force.

What do you give a dinosaur with big feet?
Plenty of room.

What fur do you get from a Mammoth?
As fur away as possible.

Why did the dinosaur lie down?
Because it couldn't lie up.

To which family does the Allosaurus belong?
I didn't know anyone in the street had one.

Why can't you put a dinosaur in a sandwich?
It's too heavy to lift.

First Caveman: Do you know that a
Stegosaurus will not harm you if you carry a
white stick?
Second Caveman: Maybe – but how fast do you
have to carry it?

Did you hear about the dinosaur who was sick
after eating a vicar?
Just proves that you can't keep a good
man down.

What do you get if you cross a prehistoric monster with a sleeper?
A dinosnore.

Two cavemen walked into a jungle clearing and saw an Iguanodon.
"Do you think that Iguanodon is safe?" asked one caveman.
"He's a darn sight safer than we are!" said the other.

Did dinosaurs always snore?
No, only when they were asleep.

What would an Archaeopteryx do if it
swallowed an elastic band?
Lay the same egg a dozen times.

First Caveman: I wish dinosaurs were born
without teeth.
Second Caveman: They usually are!

What fruit did the Diplodocus like?
Neck-tarines.

The local restaurant boasted that it could
serve any dish you liked. Oscar Doolittle
decided to put this to the test. He ordered
dinosaur and chips. The waiter went into the
kitchen but returned a few minutes later to
say that they could not fulfil the order. "No
dinosaur?" said Oscar.
"No, it's not that, sir," replied the waiter.
"We've run out of chips."

How do you get rid of a Mammoth skeleton?
Put it in a jumbo sale.

What do you call the divorced wife of
a Tyrannosaurus?
Tyrannosaurus's ex.

What animals used nutcrackers?
Toothless dinosaurs.

Knock, knock.
Who's there?
Terry.
Terry who?
Terry Dactyl.

What did the dinosaur say when all he had to eat was a thistle?
Thistle have to do.

What's the difference between dinosaurs
and potatoes?
You can't mash dinosaurs.

What do you get if you cross a sabre-toothed
tiger with a lemon?
A sourpuss.

What are the best steps to take when you meet an angry dinosaur?
Very long ones.

First Caveman: Where are you going with those spears?
Second Caveman: Dinosaur hunting.
First Caveman: But there aren't any dinosaurs around here!
Second Caveman: I know that. I wouldn't have to hunt for them if there were, would I?

What do you get if you cross a whale
with a duck?
Moby Duck.

Two dinosaurs were on a rubbish dump when
one of them found a can of film, which he ate.
The other one said, "Was that film good?"
"It was OK." said the first dinosaur, "But not
as good as the book."

First Triceratops: What's that creature over there?
Second Triceratops: It's a Stegosaurus.
First Triceratops: I wouldn't like to have to live with such an ugly face!

Knock, knock.
Who's there?
Diana.
Diana who?
Diana Saur.

What do you do when a Stegosaurus sits in front of you at the pictures?
Miss the film.

What do you call a rich dinosaur?
A gold-blooded reptile.

Why did Archaeopteryx lay eggs?
Because if they dropped them, they
would break.

Judge: You have been found guilty of stealing
an Iguanodon skeleton from the Natural
History Museum. Why did you steal it?
Criminal: My father once told me, if you're
going to steal, then steal big.

Which dinosaur ate tortillas.
Tyrannosaurus Mex.

Why did the dinosaur climb onto the roof of
the restaurant?
Because they advertised a free meal on
the house.

How can you tell there is a dinosaur in
your fridge?
You can't shut the door.

What did the Archaeopteryx eat?
Anything that fitted the bill.

What happened to the sabre-toothed tiger
when he ate a duck?
He felt down in the mouth.

What do you get if you cross a snowball with
a Tyrannosaurus?
Frostbite.

Caveman: I once went hunting dinosaurs with just one club.
Cavewoman: You must be really brave.
Caveman: Not really, there were 50 of us in the club.

Why didn't the fossil cross the road?
He didn't have the guts.

How do we know that dinosaurs were gossips?
Because most of them carried tails.

What is large and grey, and drinks from the
wrong side of a glass?
A dinosaur with hiccoughs.

What do you get if you cross a dinosaur
with a flower?
I don't know, but don't try smelling it!

What did the river say when a Tyrannosaurus
sat in it.
Well, I'm dammed.

Did you hear about the dinosaur who only
ate beans?
Human beans.

Which dinosaurs were body builders?
Tyrannosaurus pecs.

The caveman was doing a strange dance
outside the mouth of his cave when a friend
came along.
"What are you dancing for?" asked the friend.
"It's to keep the dinosaurs away." the
dancer replied.
"But there are no dinosaurs around here."
"That just proves that my dancing does
the trick."

What animal did the Stegosaurus become when
he caught a cold.
A little hoarse.

Two dinosaurs where walking through
the jungle when they saw a flock of
green budgerigars.
The first dinosaur said, "What type of birds
are those?"
The second dinosaur replied, "Unripe canaries."

Name ten prehistoric animals in five seconds.
Nine dinosaurs and a Mammoth.

What Mammoth was a famous
orchestra conductor?
Tuskanini.

What goes clomp, clomp, clomp, squish?
A Mammoth with a wet sneaker.

Why did the dinosaur walk over the hill?
Because he couldn't walk under it.

What goes squish, squish, squish, clomp?
A Mammoth with three wet sneakers.

First Caveman: Let's go home. We haven't hit a single dinosaur all day.
Second Caveman: Oh, let's miss a couple more first.

Niamh: What did dinosaurs eat?
Sian: Anything they could find.
Niamh: But what if they couldn't find anything?
Sian: Then they'd eat something else.

Searching for prehistoric creatures in the Lost Valley of the Amazon Forest, a palaeontologist suddenly came face to face with a living dinosaur, but he didn't turn a hair. He was bald.

What do you get if you cross a light bulb with
an Ichthyosaurus?
An electric ray.

Who did the Diplodocus marry?
The girl necks door.

Two cavemen were out hunting dinosaurs when the biggest Tyrannosaurus rex they had ever seen suddenly lurched out of the undergrowth in front of them.

"Don't panic," said the first caveman. "Remember what our wise man said, 'if you stand perfectly still and stare out a Tyrannosaurus it will turn tail and run away.' "

"I know what the wise man said," replied the second cavemen. "And you know what the wise man said. But does the Tyrannosaurus know what the wise man said?"

What did dinosaurs use to pay their bills?
Tyrannosaurus cheques.

What happened to the dinosaur that stood out in the rain?
Stegosaur-rust.

What dinosaur ate and drank with its tail?
All did. No animal takes off its tail when
eating or drinking.

The massive Tyrannosaurus looked down at the
tiny mouse and said: "You are the puniest, most
insignificant thing I have ever seen."
"Excuse me a second while I write that
down," said the mouse. "I want to say it to a
flea I know."

A palaeontologist and his wife were searching for dinosaurs in the Lost Valley of the Amazon Forest when an enormous Archaeopteryx swooped from the sky and carried the woman off. "Shoot, shoot!" she yelled to her husband. "I can't!" he replied "I've run out of film."

Can a toothless Tyrannosaurus bite you?
No, but he can give you a nasty suck.

What's the difference between a chicken and
a Mammoth?
About five tons.

What's the difference between a Mammoth
and a flea?
A Mammoth could have fleas but a flea can't
have Mammoths.

What did the flea say when he walked over a
dinosaur's back and reached the tail?
"This is the end."

. . . and so it is!